PIZZA

+50 Recipes for Delicious Homemade Pizza

Antonio Caputo

All rights reserved.

Disclaimer

Contents

Barbecue Chicken Pizza

- Either all-purpose flour for the pizza peel or nonstick spray f
- One recipe homemade dough
- 6 tablespoons barbecue sauce (use any variety you prefer, hot to mild)
- 4 ounces ($^1/4$ pound) smoked provolone or smoked Swiss, shredded
- 1 cup chopped, cooked chicken meat
- 1/2 small red onion, diced (about $^1/2$ cup)
- 1 teaspoon minced oregano leaves or $^1/2$ teaspoon dried oregano
- 1 ounce Parmigiana, finely grated
- 1/2 teaspoon red pepper flakes, optional

Fresh dough on a pizza stone. First, lightly dust a pizza peel with flour. Add the dough and form it into a large circle by first dimpling it with your fingertips, then picking it up by its edge and shaping it with your hands into a circle about 14 inches in diameter. Set the dough floured side down onto the peel.

Fresh dough on a pizza tray . Grease either with nonstick spray and lay the dough in a mound at the center of the tray or baking sheet. Dimple the

dough with your fingertips, then pull and press the dough until it forms a circle about 14 inches in diameter on the tray or an irregular rectangle, about 13 × 7 inches, on the baking sheet.

A baked crust. Place it on a pizza peel if using a pizza stone—or place the baked crust right on a pizza tray .

Use a rubber spatula to spread the barbecue sauce evenly over the prepared dough, leaving a 1 /2-inch border at the edge. Top with the shredded, smoked cheese.

Arrange the chicken pieces over the cheese, then sprinkle with the diced onion and oregano.

Top with the grated Parmigiana and the red pepper flakes, if using. Slide the pie from the peel to the very hot stone—or place the pizza tray with its pie either right in the oven or on the portion of the grill's grate that is not directly over the heat source.

Bake or grill with the lid closed until the crust is golden and the cheese has melted and even begun to brown lightly, 16 to 18 minutes. Slip the peel back under the crust to remove it from the stone or transfer the pizza tray or the flour sheet with

the pie to a wire rack. Set the pie aside to cool for 5 minutes be-fore slicing and serving.

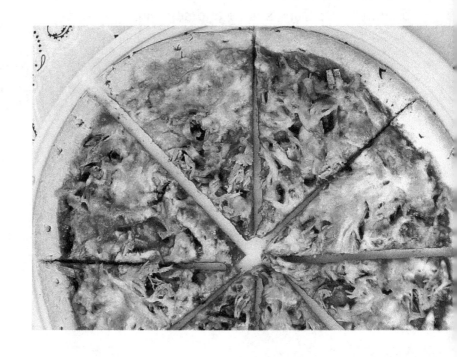

BEEF AND MUSHROOM PIZZA

- All- purpose flour for dusting the pizza peel or nonstick spray for greasing the pizza tray
- One recipe homemade dough
- 1 tablespoon unsalted butter
- 1 small yellow onion, chopped (about $1/2$ cup)
- 5 ounces cremini or white button mushrooms, thinly sliced (about $1^1/2$ cups)
- 8 ounces ($1/2$ pound) lean ground beef
- 2 tablespoons dry sherry, dry vermouth, or dry white wine
- 1 tablespoon minced parsley leaves
- 2 teaspoons Worcestershire sauce
- 1 teaspoon stemmed thyme leaves or $1/2$ teaspoon dried thyme
- 1 teaspoon minced sage leaves or $1/2$ teaspoon dried sage
- 1/2 teaspoon salt
- /2 teaspoon freshly ground black pepper 2 tablespoons bottled steak sauce
- 6 ounces Cheddar, shredded

Fresh dough on a pizza stone. Dust a pizza peel with flour. Set the dough on it and use your fingertips to dimple the dough into a large circle. Pick up the dough by its edge and turn it in your hands until it's a circle about 14 inches in diameter. Set the shaped dough floured side down on the peel.

Fresh dough on a pizza tray . Grease either with nonstick spray. Lay the dough on the tray or baking sheet dimple it with your fingertips— then pull and press it until it forms a 14-inch circle on the tray or an irregular 12 × 7-inch rectangle on the baking sheet.

A baked crust. Place it on a pizza peel if using a pizza stone—or place the baked crust right on a pizza tray .

Melt the butter in a large skillet set over medium heat. Add the onion cook, stirring often, until softened, about 2 minutes.

Add the mushrooms continue cooking, stirring occasionally, until they soften, give off their liquid, and it evaporates to a glaze, about 5 minutes.

Crumble in the ground beef cook, stirring occasionally, until well browned and cooked through, about 4 minutes.

Stir in the sherry, or its substitute, the parsley, Worcestershire sauce, thyme, sage, salt, and pepper. Continue cooking, stirring constantly, until the skillet is again dry. Set aside off the heat.

Spread the steak sauce evenly over the crust, leaving a 1 /2-inch border at the edge. Top with the shredded Cheddar, keeping that border clean.

Spoon and spread the ground beef mixture evenly over the cheese. Then slip the pizza from the peel to the hot stone—or place the pie on its pizza tray or flour sheet either in the oven or over the unheated portion of the grill grate.

Bake or grill with the lid closed until the cheese has begun to bubble and the crust is brown at its edge and somewhat firm to the touch, 16 to 18 minutes. Make sure you pop any air bubbles that arise on fresh dough, particularly at the edge and particularly during the fi rst 10 minutes of baking. Slide the peel back under the crust, taking care not to dislodge the topping, and then set aside for 5 minutes—or place the pizza on the pizza tray on a wire rack for the same amount of time before slicing and serving. Because the top-pings are especially heavy, it may not be possible to remove the pizza easily from the peel, tray, or baking sheet before slicing. If using a nonstick tray or baking sheet, carefully transfer the whole pie to a cutting board to avoid nicking the nonstick surface.

Broccoli and Cheese Sauce Pizza

- All- purpose flour for dusting a pizza peel or nonstick spray for greasing a pizza tray
- One recipe homemade dough
- 2 tablespoons unsalted butter
- 2 tablespoons all-purpose flour
- $1^1/4$ cups regular, low-fat, or fat-free milk
- 6 ounces Cheddar, shredded
- 1 teaspoon Dijon mustard
- 1 teaspoon stemmed thyme leaves or $^1/2$ teaspoon dried thyme
- 1/2 teaspoon salt
- Several dashes hot red pepper sauce
- 3 cups fresh broccoli florets, steamed or frozen broccoli florets, thawed (
- 2 ounces Parmigiana or Grana Padano, finely grated

Fresh dough on a pizza stone. Dust a pizza peel with flour. Place the dough in the peel's center and form the dough into a large circle by dimpling it with your fi n-gertips. Pick up the dough and rotate it by holding its edge, pulling it slightly as you do so, until the crust is a circle about 14 inches in diameter. Set it floured side down on the peel.

Fresh dough on a pizza tray . Grease one or the other with nonstick spray. Lay the dough on the tray or baking sheet dimple the dough with your fingertips until it's a flattened circle. Melt the butter in a large saucepan set over medium heat. Whisk in the flour until smooth and the resulting mixture becomes very light blond, about 1 minute.

Reduce the heat to medium-low and whisk in the milk, pouring it in a slow, steady stream into the butter and flour mixture. Continue whisking over the heat until thickened, like melted ice cream, perhaps a little thinner, about 3 minutes or at the first sign of a simmer. Remove the pan from the heat and whisk in the shredded Cheddar, mustard, thyme, salt, and hot red pepper sauce (to taste). Cool for 10 to 15 minutes, whisking occasionally.

If you're working with a baked crust, skip this step. If you're using fresh dough, slide the shaped but not yet topped crust from the peel to the hot stone or place the crust on its tray or baking sheet either in the oven or over the un-heated portion of the grill grate. Bake or grill with the lid closed until the crust is light brown, taking care to pop any air bubbles that arise across its surface or at its edge, about 12 minutes. Slide the peel back under the crust to remove it from the stone—or transfer the pizza tray with the crust to a wire rack.

Spread the thick cheese sauce over the crust, leaving a 1 /2-inch border at the edge. Top with the broccoli florets, arranging them evenly over the sauce. Sprinkle with the grated Parmigiana.

BROCCOLI AND TOMATO SAUCE PIZZA

- Either yellow cornmeal for dusting a pizza peel or olive oil for greasing a pizza tray
- One recipe homemade dough
- 1 large jarred pimiento or roasted red pepper
- 1/2 teaspoon red pepper flakes
- 1/2 cup Classic Pizza Sauce
- 3 ounces mozzarella, shredded
- 3 ounces provolone, Muenster, or Havarti, shredded
- 2 cups frozen broccoli florets or fresh florets, steamed
- 1 ounce Parmigiana or Grana Padano, finely grated

Fresh dough on a pizza stone. Dust a pizza peel with cornmeal. Place the dough as a lump on the peel and then dimple it with your fingertips until it's a large circle. Pick up the dough, hold it by its edge in both hands, and rotate it, stretch-ing slightly, until it's a circle about 14 inches in diameter. Set it cornmeal side down on the peel. If you've used the Spelt Pizza Dough, it may be too fragile to shape with this technique

Fresh dough on a pizza tray . Grease the tray or baking sheet with olive oil. Lay the dough on either and dimple it with your fingertips—then pull and press the dough until it forms a 14-inch circle on the tray or an irregular rectangle, 13 inches long by 7 inches wide, on the baking sheet. A baked crust. Place it on a floured pizza peel if using a pizza stone—or place the baked crust right on a pizza tray .

Puree the pimiento with the red pepper flakes in a mini food processor until smooth. Alternatively, grind them in a mortar with a pestle until a smooth paste. Set aside. Spread the pizza sauce evenly over the prepared crust, leaving a 1 /2-inch border at the edge. Top with both shredded cheeses, keeping that border intact.

Sprinkle the broccoli florets around the pie, again leaving that border intact. Dot the pimiento puree over the top, using about 1 teaspoon for each dollop. Top with the finely grated Parmigiana. Carefully slide the pizza from the peel onto the hot stone—or if you've used a pizza tray or baking sheet, place either with its pie in the oven or over the unheated portion of the grill grate.

Bake or grill with the lid closed until the cheese has melted, the red sauce is thick, and the crust is golden brown and firm to the touch, 16 to 18 minutes.

Either slip the peel back under the pizza to take it off the very hot stone or transfer the pizza on its tray or baking sheet to a wire rack. If you want to ensure the crust stays crisp, remove the pie from the peel, tray, or baking sheet after it's cooled for about 1 minute place the pizza directly on the wire rack. In any case, cool for a total of 5 minutes before slicing.

Buffalo Chicken Pizza

- Either yellow cornmeal to dust a pizza peel or unsalted butter to grease a pizza tray
- One recipe homemade dough
- 1 tablespoon unsalted butter
- 10 ounces boneless skinless chicken breasts, thinly sliced
- 1 tablespoon hot red pepper sauce, preferably Tabasco
- 1 tablespoon Worcestershire sauce
- 6 tablespoons bottled chile sauce, such as Heinz
- 3 ounces mozzarella, shredded
- 3 ounces Monterey Jack, shredded
- 3 medium celery ribs, thinly sliced
- 2 ounces blue cheese, such as Gorgonzola, Danish blue, or Roquefort

Fresh dough on a pizza stone. Dust a pizza peel with cornmeal. Place the dough in the peel's center and form the dough into a large circle by dimpling it with your fingertips. Pick up the dough and shape it with your hands, holding its edge, slowly turning the dough until it's a circle about 14 inches in diameter. Set it cornmeal side down on the peel.

Fresh dough on a baking sheet. Smear a little unsalted butter on a paper towel, then rub this around a pizza tray to grease it thoroughly. Lay the dough on the tray or baking sheet dimple the dough with your fingertips until it's a flattened circle. Then pull and press it until it forms a 14-inch circle on the tray or an irregular 12 × 7-inch rectangle on the baking sheet. A baked crust. Place it on a cornmeal-dusted pizza peel if using a pizza stone—or place the baked crust on a buttered pizza tray or large baking sheet.

Melt the butter in a large skillet or wok set over medium heat. Add the sliced chicken cook, stirring often, until cooked through, about 5 minutes. Remove the skillet or wok from the heat and stir in the hot red pepper sauce and the Worcestershire sauce. Spread the chile sauce over the crust, taking care to leave a 1/2-inch border at the edge. Lay the coated sliced chicken over the sauce.

Top with the shredded mozzarella and Monterey Jack, preserving the edge of the crust. Sprinkle the sliced celery evenly over the pie. Finally, crumble the blue cheese evenly in little dribs and drabs all over the other toppings.

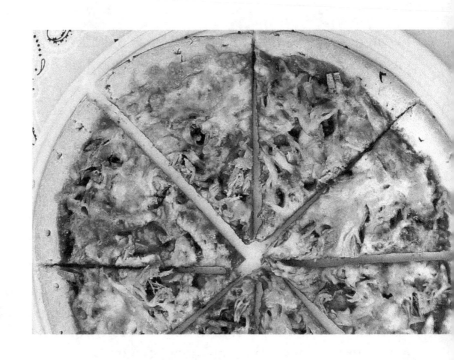

CHARD AND BLUE CHEESE PIZZA

- Yellow cornmeal for the peel or nonstick spray for the pizza tray or baking sheet
- One recipe homemade dough,
- 2 tablespoons unsalted butter
- 3 garlic cloves, minced
- 4 cups tightly packed, shredded, stemmed Swiss chard leaves
- 6 ounces mozzarella, shredded
- 1/3 cup crumbled Gorgonzola, Danish blue, or Roquefort
- 1/2 teaspoon grated nutmeg
- Up to $1/2$ teaspoon red pepper flakes, optional

Fresh pizza dough on a pizza stone. Dust a pizza peel with cornmeal, then set the dough at its center. Form it into a large circle by dimpling it with your fingertips. Pick it up and shape it with your hands, holding its edge, slowly turning the dough until it's about 14 inches in diameter. Set it floured side down on the peel.

Fresh dough on a pizza tray . Grease either one with non-stick spray. Lay the dough on the tray or baking sheet and dimple the dough with your fingertips—then pull and press it until it forms a

14-inch circle on the tray or a 12 × 7-inch irregular rectangle on the baking sheet.

A baked crust. Place it on a pizza peel if using a pizza stone—or place the baked crust right on a pizza tray .

Heat the butter in a large skillet over medium heat. Add the garlic and cook for 1 minute.

Add the greens and cook, tossing often with tongs or two forks, until soft and wilted, about 4 minutes. Set aside.

Sprinkle the shredded mozzarella over the dough, leaving a 1 /2-inch border around the edge.

Top with the greens mixture from the skillet, then sprinkle the blue cheese over the pizza. Grate the nutmeg over the top and sprinkle on the red pepper flakes, if desired.

Slip the pizza from the peel to the hot stone or place the pie on its tray or flour sheet either in the oven or on the unheated section of the grill. Bake or grill with the lid closed until the cheese has melted and is bubbling and the crust is firm to the touch, 16 to 18 minutes. Slip the peel back under the pie to take it off the hot stone, then set it aside—or transfer the pie on its tray or baking sheet to a wire rack. Cool for 5 minutes before slicing.

CHORIZO AND RED PEPPER PIZZA

- Either all-purpose flour for dusting the peel or nonstick spray for greasing the pizza tray
- One recipe homemade dough,
- 1 medium red bell pepper
- sun- dried tomatoes packed in oil
- 1 garlic clove, quartered
- ounces mozzarella or Monterey Jack, shredded
- 4 ounces ($1/4$ pound) ready-to-eat Spanish chorizo, thinly sliced
- 1/2 cup sliced pitted green olives
- 3 ounces Manchego or Parmigiana, shaved into thin strips

Fresh dough on a pizza stone. Start out by dusting a pizza peel with flour, then set the dough at its center. Use your fingertips to dimple the dough, spreading it out a bit until it's a flattened circle. Pick it up and shape it by holding its edge and slowly turning it until it's about 14 inches in diameter. Set it floured side down on the peel.

Fresh dough on a baking sheet. Grease a pizza tray with non-stick spray. Lay the dough on the tray or baking sheet dimple it with your fi nger-tips until it's a flattened circle—then pull and press it until it forms a 14-inch circle on the tray or an irregular 12 × 17-inch rectangle on the baking sheet. A baked crust. Place it on a floured pizza peel if using a pizza stone—or place the baked crust right on a pizza tray .

If you have a gas cooktop, hold the pepper with a pair of flame-safe tongs over the open flame of one of the burners until blackened all over, turning often, about 5 minutes.
Alternatively, place the pepper on a small, lipped baking sheet and broil 4 to 6 inches from a preheated broiler until blackened all around, turning occasion-ally, about 4 minutes. In either case, place the blackened pepper in a small bowl and seal tightly with plastic wrap or seal in a paper bag. Set aside for 10 minutes. (See Note.)

Peel off the outer blackened bits from the pepper. There's no need to remove every little black bit. Stem, core, and seed the pepper before tearing it into large pieces. Place these pieces in a food processor. Add the sun-dried tomatoes and garlic process until a fairly smooth paste, scraping down the sides with a rubber spatula as necessary. Spread the pepper mixture over the crust, leaving a 1 /2-inch border at the edge. Top the pepper mixture with the shredded cheese, and then arrange the chorizo slices over the pizza.

Sprinkle the olives over the pie, and then lay the shaved strips of Manchego across the toppings.

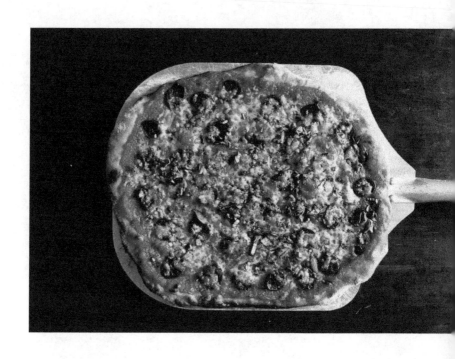

Delicata Squash and Chard Pizza

- All- purpose flour for the pizza peel or olive oil for the pizza tray
- One recipe homemade dough
- 1 tablespoon unsalted butter
- small yellow onion, chopped (about $1/2$ cup)
- cup seeded and diced delicata squash (2 or 3 medium squash)
- 4 cups chopped, stemmed Swiss chard leaves
- $1/4$ cup dry white wine or dry vermouth
- tablespoon maple syrup
- teaspoon minced sage leaves or $1/2$ teaspoon dried sage
- $1/2$ teaspoon ground cinnamon
- $1/2$ teaspoon salt
- $1/2$ teaspoon freshly ground black pepper
- 8 ounces Fontina, shredded

Fresh dough on a pizza stone. Dust a pizza peel lightly with flour. Add the dough and form it into a large circle by dimpling it with your fingertips. Pick it up with both hands at its edge and rotate it slowly, letting gravity stretch the circle while you also do so at its edge, until it's about 14 inches in diameter. Set the shaped dough floured side down on the peel.

Fresh dough on a pizza tray . Grease the tray or baking sheet lightly with a little olive oil. Lay the dough at the center and dimple the dough with your fingertips to flatten it into a thick circle—then pull and press it until it forms a 14-inch circle on the tray or an irregular 12 × 7-inch rectangle on the baking sheet.

A baked crust. Place it on a floured pizza peel if using a pizza stone—or place the baked crust on a pizza tray . Melt the butter in a large skillet set over medium heat then add the onion and cook, stirring frequently, until translucent, about 3 minutes. Stir in the diced squash and cook, stirring occasionally, for 4 minutes. Add the chopped chard and pour in the wine or vermouth. Stir constantly until partially wilted then stir in the maple syrup, sage, cinnamon, salt, and pepper.

Toss well, cover, reduce the heat to low, and cook, stirring occasionally, until the chard and squash are tender and the liquid has evaporated to a glaze, about 8 minutes. Spread the shredded Fontina evenly over the crust, leaving a 1 /2-inch border around its edge. Spoon the squash and chard topping evenly over the cheese. Slip the crust off the peel and onto the heated stone or place the pie on its tray or baking sheet in the oven or over the unheated portion of the grill. Bake or grill with the lid closed until the cheese is bubbling and the crust has turned a golden brown, 16 to 18 minutes. Slip the peel back under the crust to remove it from the stone and cool for 5 minutes, or transfer the pie on its tray or baking sheet to a wire rack to cool for 5 minutes.

Duck Confit Pizza

- All- purpose flour for the pizza peel or nonstick spray for the pizza tray
- One recipe homemade dough
- 4 ounces ($^1/4$ pound) Gruyère, shredded
- 1/3 cup canned white beans, drained and rinsed
- 1 head roasted garlic (see instructions in step 1 on page 105) or 12 roasted garlic cloves from the salad bar at the supermarket
- 2 tablespoons minced sage leaves or 1 tablespoon dried sage
- 2 teaspoons stemmed thyme leaves or 1 teaspoon dried thyme
- 1/2 teaspoon salt
- 1/2 teaspoon freshly ground black pepper
- 4 ounces duck confit legs, deboned and the meat shredded
- ounces smoked, ready-to-eat kielbasa, thinly sliced 1^1/2 ounces Parmigiana, finely grated

Fresh dough on a pizza stone. After you've dusted a pizza peel with flour, set the dough in its center and dimple the dough with your fingertips, stretching it out until it's a flattened, rippled circle. Pick it up by its edge and rotate it slowly in your hands, stretching the edge as you do so, until it's a circle about 14 inches in diameter. Set the dough floured side down on the peel.

Fresh dough on a pizza tray . Grease either with nonstick spray and set the dough in the center. Dimple the dough with your fingertips—then pull and press the dough until it forms a 14-inch circle on the tray or an irregular rectangle, about 12 inches long and 7 inches wide, on the baking sheet. A baked crust. Place it on a floured pizza peel if using a pizza stone—or place the baked crust on a greased pizza tray .

Spread the shredded Gruyère over the crust, leaving a 1 / 2-inch border at the edge. Top the cheese with the beans, then squeeze the garlic pulp out over the pizza. If you're using purchased roasted garlic, quarter the cloves so they can be sprinkled over the pie. Sprinkle with sage, thyme, salt, and pepper.

Arrange the shredded duck confit meat and the kielbasa rounds over the pie, then top with the grated Parmigiana. Slide the pie from the peel onto the heated stone or place the pie on its pizza tray either in the oven or on the unheated portion of the grill's grate.

Bake or grill with the lid closed until the crust is lightly browned and some-what fi rm to the touch, 16 to 18 minutes. If any air bubbles pop up around the edges of fresh dough, prick them with a fork.

MEATBALL PIZZA

- Either all-purpose flour for the pizza peel or olive oil for the pizza tray
- One recipe homemade dough
- 8 ounces ($1/2$ pound) lean ground beef
- 1/4 cup chopped parsley leaves
- 2 tablespoons plain dried bread crumbs
- 1/2 ounce Asiago, Grana Padano, or Pecorino, finely grated
- 2 teaspoons minced oregano leaves or 1 teaspoon dried oregano
- 1/2 teaspoon fennel seeds
- 1/4 teaspoon salt
- 1/4 teaspoon freshly ground black pepper 5 garlic cloves, minced
- 1 tablespoon olive oil
- 1 small yellow onion, chopped (about $1/2$ cup)
- One 14-ounce can crushed tomatoes
- 1 teaspoon stemmed thyme leaves or $1/2$ teaspoon dried thyme
- 1/4 teaspoon grated or ground nutmeg and 1/4 teaspoon ground cloves

- 1/4 teaspoon red pepper flakes
- 6 ounces mozzarella, shredded
- 2 ounces Parmigiana, shaved into thin strips

Fresh dough on a pizza stone. Dust a pizza peel with flour, place the dough at its center, and form the dough into a large circle by dimpling it with your fingertips. Pick it up and shape it by holding its edge and rotating it, all the while stretching it gently, until it's about 14 inches in diameter. Set it floured side down on the peel.

Fresh dough on a pizza tray. Dab a little olive oil on a paper towel and grease the tray . Lay the dough in the middle and dimple the dough with your fingertips until it's a flattened circle—then pull and press it until it forms a 14-inch circle on the tray or an irregular 12 × 7-inch rectangle on the baking sheet.

Place it on a floured pizza peel if using a pizza stone—or place the baked crust on a greased pizza tray .

Mix the ground beef, parsley, bread crumbs, the grated cheese, oregano, fennel seeds, 1 /2 teaspoon of the salt, 1 /2 teaspoon of the pepper, and 1 minced garlic clove in a large bowl until well combined. Form into 10 meatballs, using about 2 tablespoons of the mixture for each one.

Heat the olive oil in a large saucepan over medium heat. Add the onion and the remaining 4 minced garlic cloves cook, stirring often, until softened, about 3 minutes.

Stir in the crushed tomatoes, thyme, nutmeg, cloves, red pepper flakes, the remaining 1 /4 teaspoon salt, and the remaining 1 /4 teaspoon pepper. Add the meatballs and bring to a simmer.

Reduce the heat to low and simmer, uncovered, until the sauce has thickened and the meatballs are cooked through, about 20 minutes. Cool at room temperature for 20 minutes.

Spread the shredded mozzarella over the prepared crust, leaving a 1 /2-inch border at the edge. Remove the meatballs from the tomato sauce and set them aside. Spoon and spread the tomato sauce over the cheese, taking care to keep the border intact.

Cut each meatball in half and place the halves cut side down all over the pie. Top with the diced bell pepper and then the shaved Parmigiana. Slip the pizza from the peel to the hot stone or place the pizza on its tray or baking sheet either in the oven or over the unheated portion of the grill grate.

Bake or grill with the lid closed until the sauce is bubbling and the crust has turned golden brown, 16 to 18 minutes. Slide the peel back under the crust to remove it from the hot stone or transfer the pie on the tray to a wire rack. Cool for 5 minutes before slicing.

MEXICAN SHRIMP PIZZA

- All- purpose flour to dust the pizza peel or nonstick spray to grease the pizza tray
- One recipe homemade dough,
- 6 ounces medium shrimp (about 30 per pound), peeled and deveined
- 8 ounces ($1/2$ pound) cherry tomatoes, minced (see Notes)
- 1 medium shallot, minced
- $1^1/2$ tablespoons minced cilantro leaves
- 1 tablespoon extra virgin olive oil
- 1 teaspoon red wine vinegar
- 1/4 teaspoon salt
- 6 ounces Cheddar, shredded
- 1 medium jarred pickled jalapeño, seeded and minced
- 1 teaspoon cumin seeds, crushed

Fresh dough on a pizza stone. Dust a pizza peel with flour, place the dough at its center, and form the dough into a large, flattened circle by dimpling it with your fingertips. Pick it up and shape it by holding its edge and slowly turning and stretching the dough until it's about 14 inches in diameter. Set it floured side down on the peel.

Fresh dough on a pizza tray . Grease either with nonstick spray, then set the dough at the center.

Dimple the dough with your fingertips— then pull and press the dough until it forms a circle about 14 inches in diameter on the tray or an irregular 12 × 7-inch rectangle on the baking sheet. A baked crust. Place it on a pizza peel if using a pizza stone—or place the baked crust right on a pizza tray .

Fit a medium saucepan with a vegetable steamer. Add an inch of water (but not so the water rides up into the steamer) to the pan and bring the water to a boil over high heat. Add the shrimp, cover, reduce the heat to low, and steam until pink and firm, about 3 minutes. Remove and refresh under cool water to stop their cooking. Chop into bite-sized bits. Mix the cherry tomatoes, shallot, cilantro, olive oil, vinegar, and salt in a small bowl. Spread this mixture over the prepared crust, leaving a 1 /2-inch border at the rim.

Top with the shredded Cheddar, then sprinkle on the chopped shrimp, minced jalapeño, and the crushed cumin seeds. Slide the pizza from the peel to the hot stone or place the pie on its tray or baking sheet either in the oven or on the section of the grill grate that's not directly over the heat source or coals. Bake or grill with the lid closed until the crust is golden and the cheese has melted, 16 to 18 minutes. If working with fresh dough, whether homemade or store-bought, check it occasionally so you can prick any air bubbles that may arise on its surface. When the pizza's done, slip the peel back under it to get it off the stone or transfer the pie on its tray or baking sheet to a wire rack. Cool for 5 minutes before slicing and serving.

Nacho Pizza

- Yellow cornmeal for dusting the pizza peel or nonstick spray for greasing the pizza tray
- One recipe homemade dough
- $1^1/4$ cups canned refried beans
- 6 ounces Monterey Jack, shredded
- 3 medium plum tomatoes, chopped
- 1/2 teaspoon ground cumin
- teaspoon minced oregano leaves or $^1/2$ teaspoon dried oregano
- 1/2 teaspoon salt
- 1/2 teaspoon freshly ground black pepper
- 1/3 cup salsa, preferably a green (or "verde") salsa
- 1/2 cup regular or low-fat sour cream
- Jarred pickled jalapeño slices, to taste

Fresh dough on a pizza stone. Dust a pizza peel with cornmeal, place the dough at its center, and form the dough into a large circle by dimpling it with your fingertips. Pick it up and shape it with your hands at its edge, slowly turning the dough until it's about 14 inches in diameter. Set it cornmeal side down on the peel.

Fresh dough on a pizza tray . Grease the tray or baking sheet with nonstick spray. Lay the dough at the center and dimple the dough with your fingertips until it's a large, flattened circle—then pull and press it until it forms a 14-inch circle on the tray or an irregular rectangle, about 12 × 7 inches, on the baking sheet.

A baked crust. Place it on a pizza peel if using a pizza stone—or place the baked crust right on a pizza tray . Use a rubber spatula to spread the refried beans over the crust, evenly coat-ing it but leaving a 1 ⁄2-inch border at the edge. Top the beans with the shredded Monterey Jack.

Stir the chopped tomatoes, cumin, oregano, salt, and pepper in a large bowl, then spread evenly over the cheese. Dot the salsa in small spoonfuls over the crust. Slip the pizza from the peel to the heated stone or place the pie on its tray or baking sheet in the oven or on the grill grate over indirect heat. Bake or grill with the lid closed until the cheese is bubbling and the beans are hot,

Slip the peel back under the crust and set aside or transfer the pie on the tray or baking sheet to a wire rack. Cool for 5 minutes. For a crisper crust, remove the pizza from the peel, tray, or baking sheet after a minute or two to let it cool directly on the wire rack.

Top the pie with dabs of sour cream and as many jalapeño slices as you like before slicing and serving.

PEAS AND CARROTS PIZZA

- All- purpose flour for the pizza peel or nonstick spray for the pizza tray
- One recipe homemade dough
- 2 tablespoons unsalted butter
- $1^1/2$ tablespoons all- purpose flour
- 1/2 cup whole, low-fat, or fat-free milk
- 1/2 cup heavy, whipping, or light cream 3 ounces
- 2 teaspoons stemmed thyme leaves or 1 teaspoon dried thyme
- 1/2 teaspoon grated nutmeg
- cup fresh shelled peas or frozen peas, thawed
- cup diced carrots (if using frozen, then thawed)
- 3 garlic cloves, minced
- 1 ounce Parmigiana, finely grated

Fresh dough on a pizza stone. Dust a pizza peel with flour, set the dough at its center, and dimple the dough into a flattened, large circle with your fingertips. Pick it up and shape it by holding its edge, rotating it slowly and gently stretching the dough until the circle is about 14 inches in diameter. Set the dough floured side down on the peel.

Fresh dough on a pizza tray . Grease either with nonstick spray set the dough at the center of either. Dimple the dough with your fi nger-tips until it's a flattened, squashed circle—then pull and press it until it forms a 14-inch circle on the tray or a 12 × 7-inch irregular rectangle on the baking sheet. A baked crust. Place it on a floured pizza peel if using a pizza stone—or place the baked crust right on a pizza tray . Melt the butter in a large skillet set over medium heat. Whisk in the flour and continue whisking until smooth and very light beige. Whisk in the milk in a slow, steady stream then whisk in the cream. Con-tinue whisking over the heat until thick, about like fairly thin melted ice cream. Stir in the shredded cheese, thyme, and nutmeg until smooth. Cool at room temperature for 10 minutes.

Meanwhile, slip the untopped crust from the peel to the heated stone or place the crust on its tray either in the oven or over the un-heated portion of the grill grate. Bake or grill with the lid closed until the crust just begins to feel firm at its edges and just begins to brown, about 10 minutes. If you're using fresh dough, you'll need to pop any air bubbles that may arise over its surface or at its edges as it bakes. Slide the peel back under the partially baked crust and remove it from the oven or grill—or else transfer the crust on the tray or baking sheet to a wire rack.

Spread the thickened milk-based sauce over the crust, leaving a 1 /2-inch bor-der at the edge. Top the sauce with the peas and carrots, then sprinkle the garlic evenly over the pie. Finally, sprinkle the grated Parmigiana over the toppings.

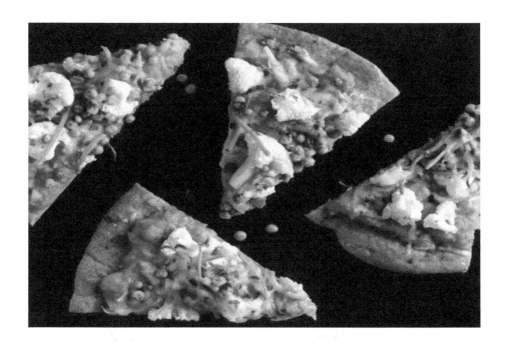

PHILLY CHEESESTEAK PIZZA

- All- purpose flour for the pizza peel or nonstick spray for the pizza tray
- One recipe homemade dough,
- 1 tablespoon unsalted butter
- 1 small yellow onion, halved through its stem and thinly sliced
- 1 small green bell pepper, seeded and very thinly sliced (
- 2 tablespoons Worcestershire sauce
- Several dashes hot red pepper sauce
- 6 tablespoons Classic Pizza Sauce (page 38), No- Cook Pizza Sauce (page 39), or jarred plain pizza sauce
- 8 ounces ($1/2$ pound) mozzarella, shredded
- 6 ounces deli roast beef, shaved paper thin and cut into strips
- 3 ounces provolone, shredded

Fresh dough on a pizza stone. Dust a pizza peel lightly with flour. Add the dough and form it into a large circle by dimpling it with your fingertips. Pick it up by its edge and shape it by slowly turning it and gently stretching it until it's about 14 inches in diameter. Set it floured side down on the peel.

Fresh dough on a pizza tray . Grease the tray or baking sheet with nonstick spray. Lay the dough at the center and dimple it with your finger-tips until it's a squashed circle—then pull and press the dough until it forms a circle about 14 inches in diameter on the tray or an irregular rectangle, about 12 × 7 inches, on the baking sheet.

A baked crust. Place it on a floured pizza peel if using a pizza stone—or place the baked crust on a pizza tray . Melt the butter in a large skillet set over medium heat. Add the onion and bell pepper cook, stirring often, until softened, about 5 minutes. Stir in the Worcestershire sauce and the hot red pepper sauce (to taste). Continue cooking until the liquid in the skillet has reduced to a glaze, about 2 more minutes. Cool at room temperature for 5 minutes. Use a rubber spatula to spread the pizza sauce over the prepared crust, leaving a 1 /2-inch border at the edge. Top with the shredded mozzarella.

Lay the roast beef strips evenly over the pie, then spoon and spread the vegetable mixture over the beef. Top with the shredded provolone.
Slip the pizza from the peel to the hot stone or place the pizza on its tray or baking sheet either in the oven or over the part of the grill grate that's not right over the heat source. Bake or grill with the lid closed until the crust is golden, evenly browned on its underside, and the cheese has melted and even begun to turn a very light brown,

about 18 minutes. Once or twice, check fresh dough, whether homemade or store-bought, to prick any air bubbles that may arise on its surface, particularly at the edge.

Polynesian Pizza

- All- purpose flour to dust the pizza peel or nonstick spray to grease the pizza tray
- One recipe homemade dough
- 3 tablespoons kecap manis or sweet thick Indonesian soy sauce (
- 6 ounces mozzarella, shredded
- 3 ounces Canadian bacon, diced
- 1 cup fresh pineapple chunks
- 1/2 cup thinly sliced scallions
- tablespoon sesame seeds

Fresh dough on a pizza stone. Dust a pizza peel with flour, set the dough at its center, and form the dough into a large, flattened circle by dimpling it with your fingertips. Pick it up by the edge and stretch it by rotating it until it's about 14 inches in diameter. Set the shaped dough floured side down on the peel.

Fresh dough on a pizza tray . Grease the tray or baking sheet with nonstick spray. Lay the dough at the center of either and dimple the dough with your fingertips—then pull and press it until it forms a 14-inch circle on the tray or an irregular 12 × 7- inch rectangle on the baking sheet.

A baked crust. Place it on a floured pizza peel if using a pizza stone—or place the baked crust on a pizza tray .

Spread the kecap manis evenly over the dough, leaving a 1 /2-inch border at the edge. Sprinkle the shredded mozzarella evenly over the sauce.

Top the pizza with the Canadian bacon, pineapple chunks, and sliced scallions—then sprinkle the sesame seeds evenly over the pie.

Slip the crust from the peel to the very hot stone or place the pie on its tray or baking sheet in the oven or on the grill over the unheated portion. Bake or grill with the lid closed until the cheese has melted and the crust is golden brown, 16 to 18 minutes.

Slip the peel back under the crust to remove it from the hot stone or transfer the pie on its tray or baking sheet to a wire rack. Cool the pizza on the peel or the baking rack for 5 minutes before slicing. To ensure that the crust stays crunchy, transfer the pizza from the peel, tray, or baking sheet right to the wire rack after a minute or so.

POT PIE PIZZA

- Yellow cornmeal for the pizza peel or nonstick spray for the pizza tray
- One recipe homemade dough
- 1 tablespoon unsalted butter
- $1^1/2$ tablespoons all-purpose flour
- 1 cup whole, low-fat, or fat-free milk, at room temperature
- 1 tablespoon Dijon mustard
- $1^1/2$ teaspoons stemmed thyme leaves or 1 teaspoon dried thyme
- 1 teaspoon minced sage leaves or $^1/2$ teaspoon dried sage
- 1 cup chopped, skinned, deboned, cooked chicken or turkey meat
- 2 cups frozen mixed vegetables, thawed
- 2 teaspoons Worcestershire sauce
- $1/2$ teaspoon salt
- $1/2$ teaspoon freshly ground black pepper
- Several dashes hot red pepper sauce
- 6 ounces Gouda, Emmental, Swiss, or Cheddar, shredded

Fresh dough on a pizza stone. Start out by dusting a pizza peel with cornmeal, then set the dough at its center. Dimple the dough with your fingertips into a large, flattened circle—then pick it up, hold it by its edge, and rotate it in front of you, all the while gently stretching it until it's about 14 inches in diameter. Set the shaped dough cornmeal side down on the peel.

Fresh dough on a pizza tray . Grease one or the other with nonstick spray. Lay the dough at the center of either and dimple the dough with your fingertips—then pull and press it until it forms a circle about 14 inches in diameter on the tray or a 12 × 7-inch irregular rectangle on the baking sheet.

A baked crust. Place it on a cornmeal-dusted pizza peel if using a pizza stone—or place the baked crust right on a pizza tray .

Melt the butter in a large saucepan over medium heat. Whisk in the flour until fairly smooth, then continue whisking over the heat until light blond, about
seconds.

Whisk in the milk in a slow, steady stream. Continue whisking over the heat until thickened, about like melted ice cream. Whisk in the mustard and herbs.

Remove the pan from the heat and stir in the meat and vegetables then stir in the Worcestershire sauce, salt, pepper, and hot red pepper sauce (to taste).

Stir in the shredded cheese until everything is uniform and coated in the sauce.

Spread evenly over the crust, leaving a 1 /2-inch border at the edge.

Slip the crust off the peel and onto the stone, or place the pie on its tray or baking sheet in the oven or over the unheated section of the grill. Bake or grill with the lid closed until the filling is bubbling and the crust has turned a golden brown and is somewhat firm to the touch, about 18 minutes. Check on a fresh-dough pie occasionally to make sure there are no air bubbles in the crust pop any that form.

Slip the peel back under the crust to remove the pie from the stone or transfer the pie on its tray or baking sheet to a wire rack. Set aside to cool for 5 minutes before slicing. If desired, transfer the pie directly to the wire rack after a minute or so to let the crust cool a bit without resting against another hot surface.

Potato, Onion, and Chutney Pizza

- All- purpose flour to dust the pizza peel or nonstick spray to grease the pizza tray
- One recipe homemade dough
- 12 ounces ($3/4$ pound) white boiling potatoes, such as Irish cobblers, peeled
- 6 tablespoons mango chutney, blueberry chutney, or another fruit-based
- chutney
- 6 ounces Monterey Jack, grated
- 3 tablespoons minced dill fronds or 1 tablespoon dried dill
- 1 large sweet onion, such as a Vidalia

Fresh dough on a pizza stone. Dust a pizza peel lightly with flour. Add the dough and form it into a large circle by dimpling it with your fingertips. Pick it up, hold its edge, and slowly rotate it, stretching it all the while, until it's about 14 inches in diameter. Set the dough floured side down on the peel.

Fresh dough on a pizza tray . Grease the tray or baking sheet with nonstick spray. Lay the dough at the center of either dimple the dough with your fingertips until it's a thick, flattened circle—then pull and press the dough until it forms a 14-inch circle on the tray or an irregular 12 × 7-inch rectangle on the baking sheet.

A baked crust. Place it on a pizza peel if using a pizza stone—or place the baked crust on a pizza tray . While the oven or grill heats, bring about 1 inch water to a boil in a large saucepan fitted with a vegetable steamer. Add the potatoes, cover, reduce the heat to medium, and steam until tender when pierced with a fork, about 10 minutes. Transfer to a colander set in the sink and cool for 5 minutes, then slice into very thin rounds.

Spread the chutney evenly over the prepared crust, leaving about a 1 /2-inch border at the edge. Top evenly with the grated Monterey Jack. Arrange the potato slices evenly and decoratively over the pie, then sprinkle with the dill. Slice the onion in half through its stem. Set it cut side down on your cutting board and use a very sharp knife to make paper-thin slices. Separate these slices into their individual strips and lay these over the pie.

Slide the pie from the peel to the very hot stone, taking care to keep the top-pings in place or place the pie on its tray or baking sheet either in the oven or on the section of the grill's grate that's not directly over the heat source. Bake or grill with the lid closed until the crust is lightly browned at its edge, even more darkly browned on its underside, 16 to 18 minutes. If any air bubbles arise at the edge or in the middle of fresh dough, pop them with a fork to produce an even crust. Slip the peel back under the hot pie on the stone or transfer the pie on its tray or baking sheet to a wire rack. Set aside to cool for 5 minutes before slicing and serving.

PROSCIUTTO AND ARUGULA PIZZA

- All- purpose flour for the pizza peel or olive oil for the pizza tray
- One recipe homemade dough
- 1/4 cup Classic Pizza Sauce (page 38), No- Cook Pizza Sauce (page 39), or jarred plain pizza sauce
- 3 ounces fresh mozzarella, thinly sliced
- 1/2 cup packed arugula leaves, thick stems removed 2 ounces prosciutto,
- tablespoon balsamic vinegar

Fresh dough on a pizza stone. Dust a pizza peel with flour, set the dough at its center, and dimple the dough into a large, flattened circle with your fingertips. Pick it up and shape it with your hands, holding the edge, slowly turning it and stretching it until it's about 14 inches in diameter. Set the shaped dough floured side down on the peel.

Fresh dough on a pizza tray . Grease either lightly with some olive oil dabbed on a paper towel. Lay the dough on the tray or baking sheet dimple the dough with your fingertips—then pull and press it until it forms a 14-inch circle on the tray or a 12 ×

7-inch rather irregular rectangle on the baking sheet.

Place it on a floured pizza peel if using a pizza stone—or place the baked crust on a pizza tray. Spread the pizza sauce evenly over the crust, leaving a 1 /2-inch border at the edge. Arrange the mozzarella slices evenly over the pie, keeping that border clean.

Lay the arugula leaves over the pie, then top with the prosciutto strips. Slip the pizza from the peel to the hot stone or place the pie on its tray or baking sheet with the pizza either in the oven or on the section of the grill grate that's not directly over the heat source.

Bake or grill with the lid closed until the crust is golden as well as somewhat firm and the cheese has melted, 14 to 16 minutes. If working with fresh dough, check it during the fi rst 10 minutes so you can pop any bubbles that may arise, particularly at the edge. Slip the peel back under the hot pie to take it off the stone or transfer the pie on its tray or baking sheet to a wire rack. Drizzle the pie with the balsamic vinegar, and then set aside to cool for 5 minutes before slicing.

REUBEN PIZZA

- Either all-purpose flour for the peel or nonstick spray for the pizza tray or baking sheet
- One recipe homemade dough
- 3 tablespoons deli mustard
- 1 cup drained sauerkraut, squeezed in batches over the sink to remove excess moisture (
- 6 ounces Swiss, Emmental, Jarlsberg, or Jarlsberg Light, shredded
- 4 ounces ($1/4$ pound) cooked deli corned beef, cut into thick slices and chopped

Fresh dough on a pizza stone. Dust a pizza peel with flour set the dough at its center. Form the dough into a large circle by dimpling it with your fingertips.

Pick it up and shape it with your hands, holding its edge, slowly turning the dough and gently stretching its edge until it's about 14 inches in diameter. Set it floured side down on the peel.

Fresh dough on a pizza tray . Grease either one with non-stick spray. Lay the dough at the center of either and dimple the dough with your fingertips until it's a thick, flattened circle—then pull and press the dough until it forms a 14-inch circle on the pizza tray or an irregular 12 × 7-inch rectangle on the baking sheet.

A baked crust. Place it on a pizza peel if using a pizza stone—or place the baked crust right on a pizza tray .

Spread the mustard evenly over the prepared crust, leaving a 1 ∕2-inch border at the edge. Spread the sauerkraut evenly over the mustard.

Top the pie with the shredded cheese, then the chopped corned beef. Care-fully slide the pizza from the peel to the heated stone or place the pie on its tray or baking sheet in the oven or over the portion of the grill grate not directly over the heat or coals.

Bake or grill with the lid closed until the crust has firmed up and turned golden and until the cheese has melted and browned a little, 16 to 18 minutes. If any air bubbles arise on fresh dough, particularly at its edge, pop them for an even crust. Slip the peel back under the pizza, taking care not to dislodge the topping, to remove the pie from the hot stone or transfer the pie on its tray or baking sheet to a wire rack. Set aside to cool for 5 minutes before slicing and serving.

Roasted Roots Pizza

- All- purpose flour for dusting the pizza peel or olive oil for greasing the pizza tray
- One recipe homemade dough
- 1/2 large garlic head (about 8 cloves, unpeeled)
- 1/2 small sweet potato, peeled, halved lengthwise, and thinly sliced
- 1/2 small fennel bulb, halved, trimmed, and thinly sliced
- 1/2 small parsnip, peeled, halved lengthwise, and thinly sliced
- tablespoon olive oil
- 1/2 teaspoon salt
- 4 ounces (^{1}/4 pound) mozzarella, shredded
- ounce Parmigiana, finely grated
- tablespoon syrupy balsamic vinegar

Fresh dough on a pizza stone. Dust a pizza peel lightly with flour. Add the dough and form it into a large circle by dimpling it with your fingertips. Pick it up, hold it by its edge with both hands, and slowly rotate it, stretching the edge a little each time, until the circle is about 14 inches in diameter. Set floured side down on the peel.

Fresh dough on a pizza tray . Grease the tray or baking sheet with some olive oil dabbed on a paper towel. Lay the dough at the center of ei-ther dimple the dough with your fingertips—then pull and press it until it forms a 14-inch circle on the tray or an irregular rectangle, about 12 × 7 inches, on the baking sheet.

A baked crust. Place it on a floured pizza peel if using a pizza stone—or place the baked crust right on a pizza tray .

Wrap the unpeeled garlic cloves in a small aluminum foil packet and bake or grill directly over the heat for 40 minutes.

Meanwhile, toss the sweet potato, fennel, and parsnip in a large bowl with the olive oil and salt. Pour the contents of the bowl onto a large baking sheet. Place in the oven or over the unheated section of the grill and roast, turning oc-casionally, until soft and sweet, 15 to 20 minutes.

Transfer the garlic to a cutting board open the packet, taking care to mind the steam. Also set the baking sheet with the vegetables aside on a wire rack.

Increase the oven's or gas grill's temperature to 450°F, or add a few more coals to the charcoal grill to raise the heat slightly.

Spread the shredded mozzarella over the prepared crust, leaving a 1/2-inch border at the edge. Top the cheese with all the vegetables squeeze the pulpy, soft garlic out of its papery hulls and onto the pie. Top with the grated Parmigiana.

Slide the pizza from the peel to the hot stone or place the pizza on its tray or baking sheet either in the oven or over the unheated section of the grill. Bake or grill with the lid closed until the crust has turned golden brown and even darkened a bit on its bottom, until the cheese has melted and started to brown, 16 to minutes. Fresh dough may develop some air bubbles during the first 10 minutes; particularly at its edge pop these with a fork to assure an even crust.

Slide the peel back under the crust to take it off the hot stone or transfer the pizza on its tray or baking sheet to a wire rack. Set aside for 5 minutes. To keep the crust crunchy, you might want to transfer the pie from the peel, tray, or flour sheet right onto the wire rack to cool after a minute or so. Once cooled a bit, drizzle the pie with the balsamic vinegar, then slice into wedges to serve.

Sausage and Apple Pizza

- Yellow cornmeal to dust the pizza peel or nonstick spray to grease the pizza tray
- One recipe homemade dough,
- 1 tablespoon olive oil
- ounces ($1/2$ pound) chicken or turkey sausage
- 1 tablespoon coarse-ground mustard
- 6 ounces Fontina, shredded
- 1 small green apple, preferably a tart apple like a Granny Smith, peeled, cored, and thinly sliced
- 2 tablespoons chopped rosemary leaves, or parsley leaves, or stemmed thyme leaves, or a combination of any two to equal 2 tablespoons
- $1^1/2$ ounces Parmigiana, Pecorino, or Grana Padano, finely grated

Fresh dough on a pizza stone. Dust a pizza peel lightly with cornmeal. Add the dough and form it into a large circle by dimpling it with your fingertips. Pick it up and shape it by holding its edge in both hands, rotating it slowly, and stretching it gently all the while, until the circle is about 14 inches in diameter. Set the dough cornmeal side down on the peel.

Fresh dough on a pizza tray . Grease one or the other with nonstick spray. Lay the dough at the center of either dimple the dough with your fingertips until it's a thick, flat circle. Then pull and press it until it forms a 14-inch circle on the tray or a 12 × 7-inch irregular rectangle on the baking sheet.

A baked crust. Place it on a cornmeal-dusted pizza peel if using a pizza stone—or place the baked crust on a pizza tray . Heat a large skillet over medium heat. Swirl in the olive oil, then add the sau-sage. Cook, turning occasionally, until well browned on all sides and cooked through. Transfer to a cutting board and slice into thin rounds. Spread the mustard evenly over the prepared crust, leaving a 1 /2-inch border at the edge. Top with the shredded Fontina, then lay the sliced sausage evenly over the pie. Tuck the apple slices among the sausage rounds, then sprinkle with one of the chopped herbs and the grated cheese.

Slip the pizza from the peel to the very hot stone if you've used a pizza tray or a baking sheet, place it with the pie in the oven or over the unheated section of the grill. Bake or grill with the lid closed until the cheese has melted and is bubbling and the crust has begun to turn golden brown at its edges, even a darker brown on its underside, 16 to 18 minutes. If working with fresh dough, pop any air bubbles that arise at its edge during the first 10 minutes of baking or grilling.

Slide the peel back under the pie to take it off the stone or transfer the pie on its tray or baking sheet to a wire rack.

SHIITAKE PIZZA

- All- purpose flour for the pizza peel or nonstick spray for the pizza tray
- One recipe homemade dough,
- 8 ounces ($1/2$ pound) soft silken tofu
- 6 ounces shiitake mushroom caps, stems removed and discarded, caps thinly sliced
- 3 medium scallions, thinly sliced
- 2 teaspoons Asian red chile paste
- 2 teaspoons minced peeled fresh ginger
- 1 teaspoon regular or reduced-sodium soy sauce
- 1 teaspoon toasted sesame oil

Fresh dough on a pizza stone. Dust a pizza peel lightly with flour. Set the dough at its center and form the dough into a thick, flat circle by dimpling it with your fingertips. Pick it up, hold it by its edge with both hands, and rotate it, slowly stretching it at the edge, until the circle is about 14 inches in diameter. Set it floured side down on the peel.

Fresh dough on a pizza tray . Grease the tray or baking sheet with nonstick spray. Lay the dough on either dimple the dough with your fingertips—then pull and press it until it forms a 14-inch circle on the tray or an irregular 12 × 7-inch rectangle on the baking sheet.

A baked crust. Place it on a pizza peel if using a pizza stone—or place the baked crust right on a pizza tray .

Process the tofu in a food processor fitted with the chopping blade until smooth and creamy. Spread over the prepared crust, making sure you leave a 1 /2-inch border at its edge.

Top the tofu with the sliced mushroom caps and scallions. Sprinkle the chile paste, ginger, soy sauce, and sesame oil evenly over the toppings. Slide the pie from the peel to the hot stone or place the pie on its tray or baking sheet either in the oven or over the unheated section of the grill grate.

Bake or grill with the lid closed until the crust is golden brown and somewhat firm to the touch, 16 to 18 minutes. Check on fresh dough a few times to make sure there are no air bubbles, particularly at its edge if so, pop them with a fork to assure an even crust. Once done, slip the peel back under the pie to take it off the hot stone or transfer the pie on its tray or baking sheet to a wire rack. Set aside to cool for 5 minutes before slicing and serving.

Spinach and Ricotta Pizza

- Either all-purpose flour for dusting the pizza peel
- One recipe homemade dough
- 2 tablespoons canola oil
- 3 garlic cloves, minced
- 6 ounces baby spinach leaves
- 1/4 teaspoon grated or ground nutmeg
- 1/4 teaspoon red pepper flakes
- 1/2 cup dry white wine or dry vermouth
- 1/4 cup regular, low-fat, or fat-free ricotta
- $1^1/2$ ounces Parmigiana, finely grated
- 1/2 teaspoon salt
- 1/2 teaspoon freshly ground black pepper

Fresh dough on a pizza stone. Dust a pizza peel lightly with flour. Add the dough and form it into a large circle by dimpling it with your fingertips. Pick it up and shape it with your hands, holding its edge, slowly turning the dough and stretching its edge until it's about 14 inches in diameter. Set the dough floured side down on the peel.
Fresh dough on a pizza tray . Grease the tray or baking sheet with nonstick spray. Lay the dough on either dimple the dough with your fi nger-tips until it's a thick, flat circle—then pull and press it until

it forms a 14-inch circle on the tray or an irregular 12 × 7-inch rectangle on the baking sheet.

A baked crust. Place it on a pizza peel if using a pizza stone—or place the baked crust right on a pizza tray . Heat a large skillet over medium heat. Swirl in the oil, then add the garlic and cook for 30 seconds. Stir in the spinach, nutmeg, and red pepper flakes just until the leaves begin to wilt then pour in the wine. Cook, stirring constantly, until the spinach has thoroughly wilted and the skillet is almost dry. Remove the skillet from the heat and stir in the ricotta, grated Parmigiana, salt, and pepper until fairly smooth.

Spread the spinach mixture over the prepared crust, leaving a 1 /2-inch border at the edge. Slide the pizza from the peel to the hot stone or place the pizza on its tray or baking sheet either in the oven or over the unheated section of the grill grate.

Bake or grill with the lid closed until the filling is set and lightly browned, until the crust is somewhat firm, 16 to 18 minutes. Slide the peel back under the pizza to remove it from the hot stone or transfer the pie on its tray or baking sheet to a wire rack. Set aside to cool for 5 minutes before slicing and serving. To ensure a crunchy crust, transfer the pie from the peel, tray, or baking sheet directly to the wire rack after a couple of minutes.

Arugula Salad Pizza

- One 16 oz. package refrigerated whole grain pizza dough, or whole grain pizza dough
- Cornmeal
- 1/3 cup marinara sauce
- $1\frac{1}{2}$ teaspoons dried oregano
- 1cup shredded plant-based cheese
- 2 cups mixed fresh arugula and baby spinach
- $1\frac{1}{2}$ cups fresh cherry tomatoes (yellow), halved
- $\frac{1}{2}$ medium red bell pepper, diced
- 1 ripe medium avocado, sliced $\frac{1}{4}$ cup roasted pistachios
- 1tablespoon balsamic vinegar

Preheat the oven to 350°F. Roll out the pizza dough to fit a 14 inch pizza pan or pizza stone. Sprinkle the pan or stone with cornmeal and fit dough on top. Spread the marinara sauce onto the dough and sprinkle the oregano and plant-based cheese over it. Place the pan or stone in the oven and bake for 30 to 35 minutes, until the crust is golden and firm to the touch.

At the last minute before serving, remove the crust from the oven and top with the arugula and baby spinach, tomatoes, bell pepper, avocado, and pistachios. The greens will wilt quickly. Drizzle with the vinegar and olive oil. Serve immediately.

Avocado 'N Everything Pizza

- 2 cups buttermilk baking mix
- 1/2 cup hot water
- 1 can (8 ounces) tomato sauce
- 1/4 cup chopped green onion
- 1/2 cup shredded mozzarella cheese
- 1/2 cup sliced mushrooms
- 1/3 cup sliced ripe olives
- 1 small tomato, sliced
- 2 tablespoons olive oil
- 1 avocado, seeded, peeled and sliced Fresh basil leaves, optional

Heat oven to 425F. Stir together buttermilk mix and water with fork in small bowl. Pat or roll into 12-inch circle on ungreased baking sheet or pizza pan. Mix together tomato sauce and green onion spread over pizza dough. Top with cheese, mushrooms, olives and tomato slices. Drizzle olive oil over top. Bake 15 to 20 minutes or until edge of crust is golden brown. Remove pizza from oven and arrange avocado slices over top. Garnish with basil leaves and serve.

BBQ Chicken Pizza

- 3 boneless chicken breast halves, cooked and cubed
- 1 cup hickory flavored barbecue sauce
- 1 tablespoon honey
- 1 teaspoon molasses
- 1/3 cup brown sugar
- 1/2 bunch fresh cilantro, chopped
- 1 (12 inch) pre-baked pizza crust
- 1 cup smoked Gouda cheese, shredded
- 1 cup thinly sliced red onion

Preheat oven to 425F. In a saucepan over medium high heat, combine chicken, barbeque sauce, honey, molasses, brown sugar and cilantro. Bring to a boil. Spread chicken mixture evenly over pizza crust, and top with cheese and onions. Bake for 15 to 20 minutes, or until cheese is melted.

BBQ Strawberry Pizza

- 1 recipe pizza dough (pre-made from the grocer's is a great time saver)
- 250 grams (1 cup) boursin cheese (fine herbs and garlic)
- 2 tbsp. balsamic glaze
- 2 cups sliced strawberries
- 1/3 cup chopped basil
- pepper to taste
- 1 tbsp. olive oil to drizzle
- shaved parmesan for garnish
- Cook pizza crust on bbq (high heat) or in the oven.
- Remove from heat and spread (while hot) with boursin (or herbed cream cheese).

Sprinkle on with basil and strawberries. Drizzle with olive oil and balsamic glaze and garnish with pepper (to taste) and shaved parmesan.

Broccoli Deep Dish Pizza

- 1 pkg dry yeast
- 1 1/3 c warm water (110 to 115 degrees)
- 1 t sugar
- 3 1/2 c unbleached flour
- 1 c cake flour
- 1 1/2 t salt
- 1 c plus 2 T olive oil
- 3 t minced garlic
- (1)15-oz can tomato sauce
- (1)12-oz can tomato paste
- 2 t oregano
- 2 t basil
- 2 c sliced mushrooms Salt and pepper
- 1 lb Italian sausage (hot or sweet)
- 1/2 t crushed fennel seeds
- 2 T butter
- 8 c blanched, roughly chopped broccoli
- 1 T shortening
- 3 1/2 c grated mozzarella cheese
- 1/2 c grated Parmesan cheese

Dissolve yeast in warm water stir in sugar. Combine flours and salt, and gradually add the dissolved yeast and 1/4 cup of the oil. Knead until the texture is smooth. Put in a large bowl, cover with plastic wrap, and let rise until triple in bulk (2-3 hours).

Meanwhile, prepare the fillings. Heat 1/4 cup of the oil in a saute pan, add 2 t garlic, and cook for 30 seconds (without browning.) Stir in the tomato sauce and paste, simmer until thickened. Stir in basil and oregano, set aside to cool.

Head 2 T of the oil and saute the mushrooms until lightly browned and the liquid is evaporated. Season to taste, and set aside to cool. Remove and discard the casings from sausage, crumble and add the sausage to the pan along with fennel. Cook thoroughly, remove and cool. Heat the butter and 2 T of the oil at 1 t of garlic and stir for 30 seconds. Stir in the broccoli until coated well and any liquid is evaporated. Season to taste set aside.

When the dough has risen, punch down. Cut off about 2/5 of it and set aside. Grease a 14 x 1 1/2" deep-dish pizza pan with the shortening. On a floured board, rool out 3/5 of the dough to a 20" circle. Fit to the pan, letting the exess dough hang over the side. Brush the dough with 1 T of the oil sprinkle with salt. Sprinkle 1 c of the mozzarella over the dough. Spread the tomato sauce across the cheese, spread the mushrooms over the tomatoes, and cover with 1 c of mozzarella. Roll out the remaining dough to approximately a 14" circle. Brush the sides of the dough inside the pan with water. Fit the 14" round into the pan. Press edges (pull if necessary) against the moustened dough to seal it. Trim the overhanging dough to 1/2" and wet it again. Fold inward and crimp to form a raised rim around the pan edge. Cut a steam vent in the top layer of the dough, and brush with 1 T of the oil. Spread the sausage across the dough and cover with the broccoli. Combine the remaining cheeses and sprinkle across the broccoli drizzle with 1/4 c of oil. Bake in a preheated 425 degree oven for 30-40 minutes. Freezes well.

Buffalo Chicken Pizza Pies

- One 12-ounce package whole-wheat English muffins (6 muffins)
- 1 medium orange bell pepper, cut into $\frac{1}{4}$-inch dice (about 1 $\frac{1}{4}$ cups)
- 1 tablespoon canola oil
- 12 ounces boneless, skinless chicken breast halves, cut into $\frac{1}{2}$-inch dice
- Half a cup pasta sauce
- 1 tablespoon Buffalo sauce
- 1 tablespoon blue cheese dressing
- 1 to 1 $\frac{1}{2}$ cups shredded, part-skim mozzarella cheese

Preheat the oven to 400°F. Slice the English muffins in half and place on a baking sheet. Toast in the oven for about 5 minutes. Remove and set aside. Heat the oil in a large nonstick skillet over medium-high heat. Add the bell pepper and cook, stirring frequently, until tender, about 5 minutes.

Add the chicken and cook until no longer pink, 3 to 5 minutes. Stir in the pasta sauce, Buffalo sauce, and blue cheese dressing and mix well.

To assemble the pizzas, top each muffin half evenly with the chicken mixture. Sprinkle the cheese evenly over the top of each. Bake until the cheese melts, about 5 minutes.

California Pizza

- 1 cup olive oil
- 2 cups fresh basil leaves
- 2 cloves garlic, chopped
- 3 tablespoons pine nuts
- 1/2 cup freshly grated Parmesan cheese
- 1 onion, thinly sliced
- 1 sweet red pepper, seeded and sliced into strips
- 1 green peppers, seeded and sliced into strips
- 2 tablespoons olive oil
- 1 tablespoon water
- 1/2 pound garlic and fennel sausage or sweet Italian sausage 3 ounces goat cheese
- 10 ounces Mozzarella cheese, coarsely grated
- 2 tablespoons freshly grated Parmesan cheese
- 2 tablespoons cornmeal

Prepare dough Dissolve yeast in water and set aside. Mix flour, salt, and sugar in a bowl. Make a "well" in the center, pour in yeast solution and olive oil. Blend in the flour using a fork, working towards the outside of teh well. As dough becomes stiff, incorporate remaining flour by hand. Gather into a ball and knead eight to ten minutes on a floured board. Place in an oil-coated bowl, cover with a damp cloth, and let rise in a warm, draft-free place until doubled in size, approximately two hours.

Prepare pesto sauce using a blender or food processor. Combine all exceptp cheese. Process but do not create a puree. Stir in cheese. Set side. Saute onions and peppers in one tablespoon olive oil and water in a large skillet over medium heat. Stir frequently until peppers are soft. Drain and set aside. Brown sausage, breaking into pieces as it cooks. Drain off excess fat. Chop coarsely and set aside.

Preheat overn to 400 degrees. Spread remaining olive oil evenly over a 12--inch pizza pan. Sprinkle with cornmeal. Punch down pizza dough, flatten lightly with a rolling pin, turn and flatten with fingers. Place dough in pan and spread to edges with fingertips. Bake five minutes. Spread pesto sauce over dough. Crumble goat cheese evenly over pesto. Add onions and peppers, sausage, and cheeses. Bake 10 minutes or until crust is slightly brown and cheese is bubbly.

Caramelized Onion Pizza

- 1/4 cup olive oil for frying onions
- 6 cups thinly sliced onions (approximately 3 pounds)
- 6 garlic cloves
- 3 Tbs. fresh thyme or 1 Tbs. dried thyme
- 1 bay leaf
- salt & pepper
- 2 Tbs. oil for dribbling on top of pizza (optional)
- 1 Tbs. drained capers
- 1-1/2 Tbs. pine nuts

Heat 1/4 cup of the olive oil and add the onions, garlic, thyme and bay leaf. Cook, stirring occasionally, until most of the moisture has evaporated and the onion mixture is very soft, almost smooth, and caramelized, about 45 minutes. Discard the bay leaf and season with salt and pepper.

Cover the dough with the onion mixture, sprinkle with capers and pine nuts, and drizzle with remaining olive oil if you are using it. Bake in pre-heated 500 degree oven for 10 minutes or until golden brown. The baking time will vary depending on whether you bake on a stone, a screen or in a pan. Be sure that your oven is well pre-heated before putting pizza in.

CHEESE CALZONE

- 1 lb. ricotta cheese
- 1 cup shredded mozzarella
- pinch of black pepper
- NY Style Pizza Dough
- Preheat oven to 500F.

Take a 6 oz. dough ball and place on floured surface. Spread, with finger tips, to a 6 inch circle. Place 2/3 cup cheese

mix on one side and fold over other side. Seal with finger tips making sure no cheese mixture is in the seal. Pinch the edge to assure a tight seal. Pat calzone to even filling inside. Check seal again for leaks. Repeat with the others.

Place calzones on a lightly greased baking sheet. Cut a 1 inch slit in the top of each for venting while baking. Place in center of oven and bake for 10–12 minutes or until golden brown. Serve with your favorite tomato sauce, warmed, either on top or on the side for dipping.

CHERRY ALMOND PIZZA

- Dough
- 2 egg whites
- 125g (4oz - 3/4 cup) ground almonds
- 90g (3oz - 1/2 cup) caster sugar few drops almond essence
- 750g (1 1/2 lb) jar Morello cherries in juice
- 60g   (2oz - 1/2 cup) flaked almonds
- 3tablespoons Morel0o cherry jam icing sugar for dusting
- whipped cream, to decorate

Preheat oven to 220C (425F. Gas 7)

In a bowl, lightly whisk egg whites. Stir in ground almonds, caster sugar and almond essence. Spread the mixture evenly over pizza base.

Drain cherries, reserving juice. Spoon over pizza, reserving a few for decoration. Sprinkle with flaked almonds and bake in the oven for 20 minutes until dough is crisp and golden.

Meanwhile, in a saucepan, heat reserved juice and jam until syrupy. Dust cooked pizza with icing sugar and decorate with whipped cream and reserved cherries.

CHICAGO STYLE PIZZA

- 1 cup Pizza sauce
- 12 oz. Shredded mozzarella cheese
- 1/2 lb. Ground beef, crumbled, cooked
- 1/4 lb. Italian Sausage, crumbled, cooked
- 1/4 lb. Pork Sausage, crumbled, cooked
- 1/2 cup Pepperoni, diced
- 1/2 cup Canadian bacon, diced
- 1/2 cup Ham, diced
- 1/4 lb. Mushrooms, sliced
- 1 small Onion, sliced
- 1 Green bell pepper, seeded, sliced
- 2 oz. Grated Parmesan cheese

For dough, sprinkle yeast and sugar into warm water in small bowl let stand until foamy, about 5 minutes.

Mix flour, cornmeal, oil and salt in a large bowl make a well in the center and add yeast mixture. Stir to form a soft dough, adding more flour if necessary. Turn onto a floured board and knead until dough is supple and elastic, 7 to 10 minutes. Transfer to a large bowl, cover and let rise in a warm spot until dough has doubled, about 1 hour. Punch down.

Roll dough to a 13-inch circle. Transfer to an oiled 12-inch pizza pan, folding the excess over to make a small rim. Spread with pizza sauce sprinkle with all but a handful of the mozzarella cheese. Sprinkle with meats and vegetables. Top with remaining mozzarella and Parmesan cheese. Let rise in a warm spot about 25 minutes.

Heat oven to 475 degrees. Bake pizza until crust is golden, about 25 minutes. Let stand 5 minutes before slicing.

DEEP-DISH PIZZA

- Nonstick cooking spray, for spraying the slow cooker insert
- 8 ounces prepared pizza dough (if refrigerated, let it rise in an oiled bowl for
- 2 hours)
- 8 ounces sliced (not grated) mozzarella cheese
- 8 ounces thinly sliced pepperoni, preferably sandwich size
- 1/2 cup store-bought pizza sauce
- 1 tablespoon grated Parmesan
- 6 fresh basil leaves, cut into chiffonade
- Pinch crushed red pepper

Preheat the slow cooker on high for 20 minutes. Spray the insert with nonstick cooking spray.

On a clean surface, stretch, roll and form the dough into roughly the same shape as the slow cooker insert. The goal is a nice, thin crust. Place in the cooker and spread out if necessary. Cook on high, UNCOVERED, for 1 hour without toppings.

Shingle the mozzarella slices over the dough and up the sides about 1 inch above the crust. Overlap each slice, moving in a clockwise circle until the perimeter is covered. Place 1 more slice to cover the empty spot in the middle, if necessary. Shingle a layer of pepperoni the same way you did the cheese.

Follow with a small layer of the pizza sauce.

Sprinkle with the Parmesan.

Cook on high until the cheesy crust is dark and caramelized and the bottom is firm and brown, another hour. Carefully take out of the slow cooker using a spatula.

Garnish with the basil and crushed red pepper.

DUTCH OVEN PIZZA

- 2 pkg. crescent rolls
- 1 jar pizza sauce
- 1 1/2 lb ground beef
- 8oz shredded cheddar cheese
- 8oz shredded mozzarella cheese
- 4oz pepperoni
- 2 tsp oregano
- 1 tsp garlic powder
- 1 tsp onion powder

Brown ground beef, drain. Line Dutch oven with 1 pkg. crescent rolls. Spread pizza sauce on dough. Add ground beef, pepperoni, and sprinkle oregano, garlic powder, and onion powder on top. Add cheeses and use second pkg. crescent rolls to form top crust. Bake 30 minutes at 350 degrees. Other such as chopped green pepper, chopped

Egg Salad Pizza Cones

- 1/4 cup bottled reduced-fat creamy Italian salad dressing
- 1/2 teaspoon Italian seasoning, crushed
- 6 hard-cooked eggs, chopped
- 1/4 cup sliced green onions with tops
- 1/4 cup minced pepperoni
- 6 plain ice cream cones
- Chopped mushrooms, green peppers, black olives as desired
- 3/4 cup pizza sauce
- 2 tablespoons grated Parmesan cheese

In medium bowl, stir together dressing and seasoning. Stir in eggs, onions and pepperoni. Cover and refrigerate until ready to serve.

To serve, scoop about 1/3 cup of the mixture into each cone. Top with about 2 tablespoons pizza sauce and mushrooms, peppers and olives as desired. Sprinkle each with about 1 teaspoon cheese.

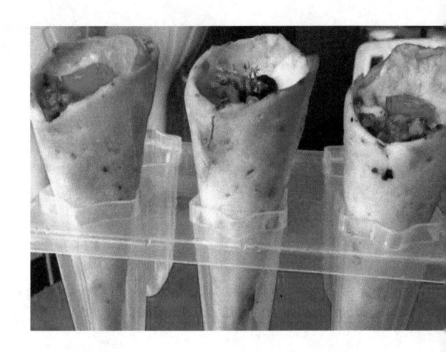

Fig, Taleggio & Radicchio Pizza

- 3 dried Mission figs
- ½ cup dry red wine
- 2 tablespoons raw walnut pieces All-purpose flour
- 1 (6 oz.) ball No-Knead Pizza Dough
- 2 tablespoons extra virgin olive oil
- ½ small head radicchio, shredded (about ¼ cup)
- 2 oz. Taleggio or another pungent cheese, cut into small pieces

Preheat the broiler with the rack set 5 inches from the element or flame. If you are using a cast-iron skillet or griddle pan for the pizza, set it over medium-high heat until it gets smoking hot, about 15 minutes. Transfer the skillet (turned upside down) or griddle pan to the broiler.

Put figs in a small skillet set over medium heat, pour in the wine, and bring to a boil. Turn off the heat and let the figs soak for at least 30 minutes. Drain, then chop into ½ inch pieces. Toast the walnut pieces in a dry skillet over medium-high heat, 3 to 4 minutes. Transfer to a plate, let cool, and then coarsely chop.

To shape the dough, dust a work surface with flour and put the ball of dough on it. Sprinkle with flour and knead a few times until the dough comes together. Add more flour if necessary. Form it into an 8 inch round by pressing from the center out toward the edges, leaving a 1 inch border thicker than the rest.

Open the oven door and quickly slide out the rack with the cooking surface on it. Pick up dough and quickly transfer it to the cooking surface, being careful not to touch the surface. Drizzle 1 tablespoon of oil onto the dough, scatter the walnut pieces on top, then radicchio, then chopped figs, and then cheese. Slide rack back into oven and close door. Broil pizza until crust has puffed up around the edges, pizza has blackened in spots, and cheese has melted, 3 to 4 minutes.

Remove pizza with a wooden or metal peel or a square of cardboard, transfer it to a cutting board, and let it rest a few minutes. Drizzle remaining 1 tablespoon of oil on top, cut the pizza into quarters, transfer it to a plate, and eat.

FROZEN PEANUT BUTTER PIZZA PIE

- 2 Thin Dough 12 inch dough shells
- 2 Tbls. butter, softened
- 1 8 oz. package cream cheese, softened
- 1 cup creamy peanut butter, softened
- 1 1/2 cups powdered sugar
- 1 cup milk
- 1 12-oz. package Cool Whip
- chocolate syrup

Preheat oven to 400°F.

Brush tops and rims of pizza shells with butter, place in center oven rack and bake 8 minutes. Remove and cool on wire racks.

In a large electric mixer bowl, beat cream cheese and peanut butter, then add the powdered sugar in three portions, alternating with the milk. Fold in thawed Cool Whip, then spread mixture over the cooled pizza crusts. Freeze until firm. Serve pizzas cold, but not frozen. Just before serving, drizzle with chocolate syrup.

GRIDDLE SUPER PIZZA

- $\frac{1}{4}$ cup marinara sauce
- $\frac{1}{4}$ cup chopped fresh spinach
- $\frac{1}{4}$ cup shredded mozzarella
- $\frac{1}{4}$ cup quartered cherry tomatoes
- 1/8 teaspoon oregano

Whisk flour, water, oil and salt together until smooth.

Pour batter onto hot griddle misted with cooking spray.

Heat each side for 4-5 minutes (until crust starts to brown).

Flip crust once more and top with marinara sauce, spinach, cheese, tomato and oregano.

Heat for 3 minutes or until cheese melts.

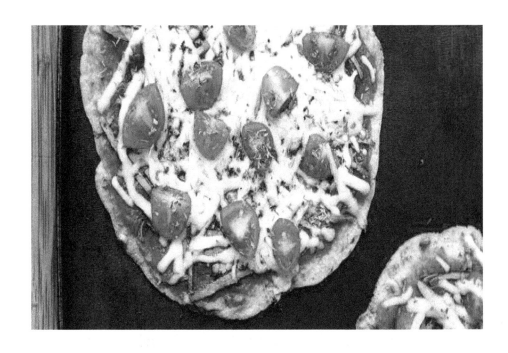

GRILLED PIZZA

- 1 teaspoon dried yeast
- 1 tablespoon soy oil
- 1 teaspoon sugar
- $\frac{1}{2}$ cup warm water (110°F)
- 1 $\frac{1}{2}$ cup bread flour
- 1 tablespoon soy flour
- 1 teaspoon salt

Combine yeast, sugar and $\frac{1}{2}$ cup very warm water in bowl, let sit for five minutes. Combine flour and salt in bowl. Mix yeast mixture with bowl containing dry . Add a little extra flour if dough is sticky. Knead for a good 10 minutes.

Put into a greased bowl and let rise for 60 minutes until it doubles in size. Turn out onto a floured surface then knead lightly until smooth. Roll out into a $\frac{1}{4}$" thick, 12" diameter circle. The thinner the dough is rolled, the better.

Before placing your crust on the grill, be sure that your grill is both clean and well oiled. This will help prevent the dough from sticking to the grill. You will need something large enough to transport your dough to the grill. A pizza spatula is highly recommended for this task. Brush an even coat of extra virgin olive oil on the side that will be facing down first. The oil will introduce flavor and help to keep the dough from sticking to the grill as well as giving the crust a nice crisp finish.

Before placing your pizza on the grill, you may want to remove the top rack of your grill to make it easier to flip your pizza. Cook the first side from 1-3 minutes before flipping depending on the heat of your grill. During this time you will need to brush olive oil on the side that is facing up. While cooking the first side, peak under the edge of the crust to monitor its finish.

Cook until you are satisfied with the finish and then flip your crust over. After flipping, immediately apply any topping that you would like. It's highly recommended that you keep the topping very light, as they will not have a chance to cook on the grill without burning the crust. You may consider precooking certain such as meats and thick vegetables. Be sure to lower the lid as soon as possible to trap the heat in and finish cooking the toppings.

Cook the pizza for an additional 2-3 minutes or until you are satisfied with the crusts finish.

Grilled White Pizza with Soppressata and Cherry Peppers

- Dough
- 1 cup olive oil
- 6 cloves smashed garlic cloves
- 2 cloves minced garlic
- 1 cup whole milk ricotta
- 1 teaspoon chopped fresh thyme
- 2 teaspoons plus 1 tablespoon chopped fresh oregano, keep separate 1/2 cup olive oil
- 4 cups shredded mozzarella
- 1 cup shredded Parmesan
- 6 ounces Soppressata or other cured salami, sliced thin
- 4 ounces cherry peppers (jarred), drained and torn into pieces
- Kosher salt and freshly ground black pepper Cornmeal (coarse ground), as needed

Preheat oven to 150°F or to the lowest setting. When oven reaches temperature, turn off the oven. Pour the water into the work bowl of a food processor or stand mixer (both should have dough attachment). Sprinkle the oil, sugar, and yeast over the water and pulse several times until mixed. Add the flour and salt and process until the mixture comes together. The dough should be soft and slightly sticky. If it is very sticky, add flour 1 tablespoon at a time, and pulse briefly. If it is still too stiff, add 1 tablespoon of water and pulse briefly. Process another 30 seconds.

Turn the dough onto a lightly floured work surface. Knead it by hand to form a smooth, round ball. Put the dough into a large, clean bowl that has been coated with olive oil and cover tightly with plastic wrap. Let is rise for 15 minutes in the oven before proceeding.

In a small pot add the 1 cup olive oil with the 6 cloves smashed garlic. Bring to a simmer, then remove from heat to allow the garlic to infuse the oil and to cool. In a small bowl combine ricotta, 2 cloves minced garlic, chopped thyme, and 2 teaspoons chopped oregano. Remove the dough from the oven, punch it down, and turn it out onto a lightly floured work surface. Divide the dough into four 4-inch balls. Place pizza stone on grill and preheat gas grill to high.

Lightly sprinkle work surface with $\frac{1}{4}$ cup cornmeal. Roll or stretch 1 dough round gently into a 12" rectangle or circle, $\frac{1}{4}$" thick. Brush with about 2 tablespoons of olive oil. Sprinkle pizza peel with cornmeal and then slide dough round onto it. Place toppings onto dough round in this order First brush with garlic oil, then dollop with herbed ricotta, then top with mozzarella, parmesan, Soppressata, and cherry peppers.

With pizza peel, slide pizza onto the hot pizza stone. Close the lid as quickly as possible. Grill for about 5-7 minutes, or until bottom of crust is well browned, the toppings are warm and the cheese is bubbly, about 5 to 10 minutes.

Grilled Vegetable Pizza

- 1-cup lukewarm water (about 100 degrees F)
- $\frac{1}{4}$ cup olive oil 1 $\frac{1}{2}$ tsp honey
- 1 envelope rapid rise yeast
- 3 cups all purpose flour, plus extra as needed
- 1 $\frac{1}{2}$ tsp kosher salt.

Preheat oven to 150 degrees or to the lowest setting. When oven reaches temperature, turn off the oven. Pour the water into the work bowl of a food processor or stand mixer (both should have dough attachment). Sprinkle the oil, sugar, and yeast over the water and pulse several times until mixed. Add the flour and salt and process until the mixture comes together. The dough should be soft and slightly sticky. If it is very sticky, add flour 1 tbsp at a time, and pulse briefly. If it is still too stiff, add 1 tbsp of water and pulse briefly. Process another 30 seconds.

Turn the dough onto a lightly floured work surface knead it by hand to form a smooth, round ball. Put the dough into a large, clean bowl that has been coated with olive oil and cover tightly with plastic wrap. Let is rise for 15 minutes in the oven before proceeding. Remove the dough from the oven, punch it down, and turn it out into a lightly floured work surface.

Divide the dough into four 4-inch balls and proceed with pizza-making instructions.

MARINARA, MOZZARELLA, ARUGULA & LEMON PIZZA

- 1 recipe Pizza Dough
- 2 cups tomato purée (straight from a jar, or whole tomatoes from a 28 oz. can, puréed)
- 1clove garlic, smashed
- 1teaspoon dried oregano
- 1teaspoon tomato paste
- $\frac{1}{2}$ teaspoon salt (Note taste the purée before adding, particularly if it was processed with salt)
- Ground black pepper
- $\frac{1}{4}$ teaspoon red pepper flakes (optional)
- 2cups shredded mozzarella cheese
- $\frac{1}{2}$ cup grated Parmigiana
- Optional but really nice
- $\frac{1}{2}$bunch (about 2 cups) arugula, cleaned and dried
- $\frac{1}{2}$lemon
- A drizzle of olive oil

Pour the tomato purée into a medium-size saucepan and heat over medium heat. Add the garlic, oregano, and tomato paste. Stir to make sure the paste has been absorbed into the puree.

Bring up to a boil (this helps sauce reduce a bit), then lower the heat and stir to make sure the sauce is not sticking. The sauce can be ready in 15 minutes or can simmer for longer, up to $\frac{1}{2}$ hour. It will reduce by about one-fourth, which gives you at least $\frac{3}{4}$ cup of purée per pizza.

Taste for salt and season accordingly, and add the black pepper and/or red pepper flakes. Remove the garlic clove.

Ladle the sauce into the middle of dough circle, and with a rubber spatula, spread until the surface is completely covered. Place the mozzarella (1 cup per 12 inch pizza) on top of the sauce. Remember, the cheese will spread as it melts in the oven, so don't worry if it seems as if your pizza is not amply covered with cheese.

Place in a preheated 500°F oven and bake as directed for the pizza dough (see details in preceding recipe). When the pizza is done, garnish it with the Parmigiana and the arugula (if using). Squeeze the lemon all over the greens and/or drizzle with olive oil if you wish.

Mexican Pizza

- 1/2 lb. ground beef
- 1/2 teaspoon salt
- 1/4 teaspoon dried minced onion
- 1/4 teaspoon paprika
- 1-1/2 teaspoon chili powder
- 2 tablespoons water
- 8 small (6-inch diameter) flour tortillas
- 1 cup Crisco shortening or cooking oil
- 1 (16 oz.) can refried beans
- 1/3 cup diced tomato
- 2/3 cup mild picante salsa
- 1 cup shredded cheddar cheese
- 1 cup shredded Monterey Jack cheese
- 1/4 cup chopped green onions
- 1/4 cup sliced black olives

Cook the ground beef over medium heat until brown, then drain off the excess fat from the pan. Add salt, onions, paprika, chili powder and water, and then let mixture simmer over medium heat for about 10 minutes. Stir often.

Heat oil or Crisco shortening in a frying pan over medium-high heat. If oil begins to smoke, it is too hot. When oil is hot, fry each tortilla for about 30-45 seconds per side and set aside on paper towels. When frying each tortilla, be sure to pop any bubbles that form so that tortilla lays flat in oil. Tortillas should become golden brown. Heat up refried beans in a small pan over the stove or in the microwave.

Preheat oven to 400F. When meat and tortillas are done, stack each pizza by first spreading about 1/3 cup refried beans on the face of one tortilla. Next spread 1/4 to 1/3 cup of meat, then another tortilla. Coat your pizzas with two tablespoons of salsa on each, then split up the tomatoes and stack them on top. Next divide up the cheese, onions and olives, stacking in that order. Place pizzas in your hot oven for 8–12 minutes or until cheese on top is melted. Makes 4 pizzas.

MINI PIZZA BAGELS

- Mini Bagels
- Pizza Sauce
- Shredded Mozzarella Cheese

Preheat oven to 400*

Split bagels in half, spread sauce evenly on each half, sprinkle cheese.

Bake 3-6 minutes or until cheese is melted to your liking.

MUFFULETTA PIZZA

- 1/2 cup finely chopped celery
- 1/3 cup chopped pimento-stuffed green olives 1/4 cup chopped pepperoncini 1/4 cup chopped cocktail onions
- 1 clove garlic, minced
- 3 Tbsp. extra virgin olive oil
- 2 tsp. dry Italian salad dressing mix
- 3 oz. thin-sliced deli ham/salami, diced
- 8 oz. shredded provolone cheese
- 2 12" uncooked dough crusts
- extra virgin olive oil

Mix first 7 for marinated olive salad and chill overnight. Combine olive salad, ham, and cheese. Top one dough crust with 1/2 of mixture. Drizzle with oil. Bake in preheated 500° F oven for

8-10 minutes or until crust is golden brown and cheese is melted. Remove from oven and cool on a wire rack for 2-3 minutes before cutting into wedges and serving. Repeat with other dough crust.

PAN PIZZA

- Dough
- 2 tablespoons olive oil
- 1 clove garlic, peeled and minced
- 2 tablespoons tomato paste
- Pinch of chile flakes, to taste
- 128-ounce can chopped or crushed tomatoes
- 2 tablespoons honey, or to taste
- 1 teaspoon kosher salt, or to taste

Make the dough a day or two before you want to bake the recipe makes enough for three pies. Combine the flour and salt in your largest mixing bowl. In another mixing bowl, combine the water, butter, olive oil and yeast. Mix well.

Use a rubber spatula to create a well in the center on the flour mixture, and add to it the liquid from the other bowl, stirring with the spatula and scraping down the sides of the bowl to bring everything together. Mix it all together until it is a large, shaggy ball of wet dough, cover with plastic wrap and allow to sit for 30 minutes.

Uncover the dough and, with floured hands, knead it until it is uniformly smooth and sticky, approximately 3 to 5 minutes. Move the dough ball into a clean mixing bowl, cover with plastic wrap and allow to rise for 3 to 5 hours at room temperature, then refrigerate, at least 6 hours and up to 24.

The morning you want to make the pizzas, remove the dough from the refrigerator, divide into 3 chunks of equal size (about 600 grams each) and shape them into oblong balls. Use olive oil to grease three 10-inch cast-iron skillets, 8-inch-by-10-inch baking pans with high sides, 7-inch-by-11-inch glass baking dishes or some combination thereof, and place the balls into them. Cover with plastic wrap, and let rise at room temperature, 3 to 5 hours. mixture is glossy and just beginning to caramelize.

Make the sauce. Place a saucepan over medium-low heat, and add to it 2 tablespoons olive oil. When the oil is shimmering, add the minced garlic and cook, stirring, until it is golden and aromatic, approximately 2 to 3 minutes.

Add the tomato paste and a pinch of chile flakes, and raise the heat to medium. Cook, stirring often

Add the tomatoes, bring to a boil, then lower heat and allow to simmer for 30 minutes, stirring occasionally.

Take sauce off the heat, and stir in the honey and salt, to taste, then blend in an immersion blender or allow to cool and use a regular blender. (The sauce can be made ahead of time and stored in the refrigerator or freezer. It makes enough for 6 or so pies.)

After 3 hours or so the dough will have almost doubled in size. Stretch the dough very gently to the sides of the pans, dimpling it softly with your fingers. The dough can then be left to rest for another 2 to 8 hours, covered with wrap.

Make the pizzas. Heat oven to 450. Gently pull the dough to the edges of the pans if it hasn't risen to the edges already. Use a spoon or ladle to put 4 to 5 tablespoons of sauce onto the dough, gently covering it entirely. Sprinkle the low-moisture mozzarella onto the pies, then dot them with the fresh mozzarella and the pepperoni to taste. Sprinkle with the oregano and lash with a little olive oil.

Place the pizzas onto the middle rack of the oven on a large baking sheet or sheets to capture spills, then cook for 15 minutes or so. Use an offset spatula to lift the pizza and check the bottoms. The pizza is done when the crust is golden and the cheese is melted and starting to brown on top, approximately 20 to 25 minutes.

Pepperoni Pizza Chili

- 2 pounds ground beef
- 1 pound Hot Italian Sausage Links
- 1 large onion, chopped
- 1 large green pepper, chopped
- 4 garlic cloves, minced
- 1 jar (16 ounces) salsa
- 1 can (16 ounces) hot chili beans, undrained
- 1 can (16 ounces) kidney beans, rinsed and drained
- 1 can (12 ounces) pizza sauce
- 1 package (8 ounces) sliced pepperoni, halved
- 1 cup water
- 2 teaspoons chili powder
- 1/2 teaspoon salt
- 1/2 teaspoon pepper
- 3 cups (12 ounces) shredded part-skim mozzarella cheese

In a Dutch oven, cook the beef, sausage, onion, green pepper and garlic over medium heat until meat is no longer pink; drain. Stir in the salsa, beans, pizza sauce, pepperoni, water, chili powder, salt and pepper. Bring to a boil. Reduce heat; cover.

Pesto Pizza

- 1 1/2 cups (packed) stemmed spinach leaves
- 1/2 cup (packed) fresh basil leaves (about 1 bunch)
- 1 1/2 tablespoons oil from oil-packed sun-dried tomatoes or olive oil
- 1 large garlic clove
- Olive Oil
- 1 12 inch NY Style dough shell
- 1/3 cup sliced drained oil-packed sun-dried tomatoes 2 cups grated mozzarella cheese (about 8 ounces)
- 1 cup grated Parmesan cheese

Blend first 4 in processor to coarse puree. Transfer pesto to small bowl. (Can be prepared 1 day ahead. Press plastic directly onto surface of pesto to cover refrigerate.) Preheat oven to 500F. Grease 12 inch pizza pan with olive oil. Arrange dough in pan and spread all of pesto over dough. Sprinkle with sun-dried tomatoes, then cheeses. Bake pizza until crust browns and cheese melts.

PHILLY CHEESESTEAK PIZZA

- 1 Medium Onion, sliced
- 1 Medium Green pepper, sliced
- 8 oz. Mushrooms, sliced
- 8 oz. Roast beef, shaved
- 3 tbls. Worchestershire sauce
- 1/4 teas. Black pepper
- 1 Batch Sicilian Thick Crust Dough
- 3 tbls. Olive oil
- 1 teas. Crushed garlic
- 4 cups provolone cheese
- 1/4 cups Parmesan cheese, grated

Saute vegetables in 1 tb. olive oil until limp add roast beef. Cook for three more minutes. Add Worchestershire sauce and pepper stir and remove from heat. Set aside. Brush prepared dough with 3 tb. olive oil and spread crushed garlic over entire surface of dough. Top with a light layer of shredded cheese, then meat/vegetable mixture, distributing evenly. Top with remaining shredded cheese, then Parmesan. Bake in prehated 500F oven until cheese is melted and bubbly. Let sit 5 minutes before cutting and serving.

PITA PIZZA WITH GREEN OLIVES, MONTEREY JACK & CHOPPED SALAD

Chopped Salad

- 1garlic clove, peeled and halved
- 2 tablespoons balsamic vinegar
- 1small red onion, halved, thinly sliced
- $\frac{1}{4}$ cup extra virgin olive oil
- Coarse sea salt and fresh black pepper 3 hearts of romaine, coarsely chopped 4 medium Kirby cucumbers, cut into
- bite-sized pieces
- 2medium tomatoes, cored, seeded, and diced
- 1 ripe avocado, diced
- 5 fresh basil leaves, torn into pieces
- 8-10 fresh mint leaves, torn into pieces

Pita Pizza

- 4 (7 inch) pocketless pita breads
- 8oz. Monterey Jack cheese, grated
- $\frac{1}{2}$ cup pitted and chopped green olives
- 2 jalapeño peppers, minced Crushed red pepper flakes Freshly milled black pepper Shaved Parmesan cheese for garnish

Place a pizza stone or an inverted rimmed baking sheet in the upper third of the oven and preheat the oven to 450°F.

To prepare the salad, vigorously rub the inside of a large bowl with the garlic. Add vinegar and red onion and set aside for 5 minutes. Whisk in the oil and season with salt and pepper. Add the lettuce, cucumber, tomato, avocado, basil, and mint and toss well. Bake the pitas, in batches if necessary, on the heated pizza stone or pan for 3 minutes. In a small bowl, combine the cheese, olives, and jalapeños. Divide this mixture among the four pitas.

Return the pitas to the oven, two at a time, and bake until the cheese is bubbling and lightly browned, about 5 minutes. Mound the salad on top of the pizzas, sprinkle with Parmesan cheese, and serve.

SPREAD pita bread with sauce. ADD extra garlic powder and oregano if desired. Then ADD your choice of toppings! Chopped tomatoes, onions, peppers, zucchini, or yellow squash are all delicious and nutritious! Top with QUICK AND EASY PIMENTO CHEESE and sliced black ripe olives. BAKE at 400° for 10 minutes.

Pizza Burgers

- 1 lb ground beef
- 1/4 c chopped olives
- 1 c cheddar cheese
- 1/2 t garlic powder
- 1 8 oz can tomato sauce
- 1 onion, diced

Brown meat with garlic and onions.

Remove from heat and stir in tomato sauce and olives.

Place in hot dog buns with cheese.

Wrap in foil and bake for 15 minutes at 350 degrees.

CPSIA information can be obtained
at www.ICGtesting.com
Printed in the USA
BVHW010755300421
605944BV00017BA/430

9 781801 977173